Financial Breakthrough

Financial Breakthrough

✦

God's Plan for Getting out of Debt

Travis Moody

iUniverse, Inc.
New York   Bloomington

Financial Breakthrough
God's Plan for Getting Out of Debt

Copyright © 2006, 2008 by Travis Moody, Sr.

iUniverse books may be ordered through booksellers or by contacting:

iUniverse
1663 Liberty Drive
Bloomington, IN 47403
www.iuniverse.com
1-800-Authors (1-800-288-4677)

ISBN: 978-1-60528-018-9 (pbk)
ISBN: 978-0-595-61445-5 (ebk)

Old book
ISBN: 978-0-595-38822-6 (pbk)
ISBN: 978-0-595-83199-9 (ebk)

Printed in the United States of America

Thanks to *The Dream Giver* for giving me a big dream. My big dream is to teach financial stewardship in order to help millions of people grow closer to Christ, live in peace, and fund God's great commission.

This book is dedicated in the memory of my father, Herbert M. D. Moody.

Contents

Acknowledgments

I never imagined writing a book. After reading *The Dream Giver* by Bruce Wilkerson, I knew that God intended for me to share my story to benefit others. I shared my dream of teaching financial stewardship to millions with my accountability partner, Pastor Dan Henley of Journey Christian Church in Bartlett, Tennessee. I accepted Dan's challenge to speak to his congregation and began to document a message from God.

I was telling a member of my local church my concerns about narrowing down God's message to a thirty-minute message. My daughter Erica overheard the conversation and commented, "Daddy, why don't you just write a book?" Erica's question helped me realize God's desire for me to write *Financial Breakthrough*.

So many people helped me in this process. I appreciate my mom, Essie Moody, and brother, Larry Moody, for their support. So many friends also provided encouragement to write this book. I sincerely thank my accountability partners, Pastor Dan Henley and Keith Holmes, who inspired me to dream and encouraged me to finish.

Jack Benson and James Levisee provided their talents with pictures and cover design. Thanks to Associate Pastor Bobby Hamilton at New Life Church in Maumelle, Arkansas, for proofreading and providing feedback on the first manuscript.

I am forever indebted to the late Larry Burkett and Howard Dayton of Crown Financial Ministry. Their message brought hope to our debt situation. Through Crown's small group class, we learned most of the lessons shared in this book. We also are thankful to our Crown small group leaders, Cameron and Marilee Walker, and to Bellevue Baptist Church in Memphis, Tennessee, for providing Crown Financial Ministry small groups.

I would like to thank several pastors who have ministered to us during our journey. They include Dr. W. R. Davis of Rocky Creek Baptist Church in Simpsonville, South Carolina; Pastor Terry Harris of Tacoma Christian Center in

Tacoma, Washington; Pastor John Fichtner of Liberty Church in Marietta, Georgia; Pastor Vince Allen of New Life International in Columbus, Georgia; Apostle Stacy Spencer at New Direction Church in Memphis, Tennessee; and Pastor Rick Bezet at New Life Church in Maumelle, Arkansas.

I would like to thank my children, Erica, Travis Jr., Donovan, and Gilana, for allowing just enough time between basketball games, homework, and piggyback rides for Daddy to finish his book.

Without a doubt, the biggest contributor to this book has been my wife, Carol, who has given me so much guidance throughout this process. She has proofread many copies and given me ideas on the title and cover. Beyond this book, Carol has been an unbelievable wife and mother. Carol is so beautiful, smart, loving, and supportive. I am amazed and so thankful that God showed me favor by placing a notion in her heart to pick me.

Preface

In 2000, God allowed Carol and me to go through a difficult financial situation. I say he allowed it because we were in the situation because of my actions. In the past God had always protected me from my own silliness. However, this time he did not. He allowed me to experience hardship.

I had always dreamed of owning a business. I had completed my MBA at one of the top business schools in the country and had a good career with a Fortune 500 company in Seattle. I had spent a couple of years researching and planning for an opportunity to buy a company. I found a small company in Atlanta that met the criteria and went after it. I quit my job in Seattle and moved to Georgia to pursue my dream. The company turned out to be difficult to buy, and the deal fell through. I spent all of our savings and the equity in our home. I used credit cards to charge living and business expenses during my four months in Atlanta and incurred legal and consulting expenses associated with buying the business. I was so presumptuous that this deal would make me rich that, in the middle of all of this, I took out a 100% mortgage for a 4,800-square-foot dream home in Atlanta.

Now there was nothing wrong with my desire to own a business or with leaving my job to pursue this dream. However, along the way I ignored God's warnings that I was stepping out of his will. He gave me uneasiness about using credit cards, but I ignored it. He provided obstacles in getting the mortgage, but I manipulated the system and even provided false information to get the loan. If I had been honest, the loan would have been denied, and I would have saved myself much heartache.

After four months of hard work, I finally came to my senses and realized that this business deal would not happen. We were left with no money, no income, and over $100,000 in debt. The home that was supposed to be our dream home became a nightmare. We had a huge mortgage on a home that we could not afford to live in, maintain, or even sell.

Carol and I had been married almost ten years at the time, but this was the first time I had seen her cry because of something I had done. I remember her saying, "Travis, people look at where we live and think that we have made it, but I cannot even afford to go to Wal-Mart to get basic needs for our family. We are living a lie." She never placed blame, but, nonetheless, this hurt me. I felt like I had failed my wife, and I felt that my God had failed me. I was mad at God. I could not understand why he allowed this to happen.

Do not get me wrong. I was not in denial. I knew it was my fault, but God had always protected me from my own foolishness. I could not understand why he did not stop me, or, better yet, why didn't he make it work out in my favor? Isn't that what the Bible says? I had always paid my tithes. I had tried to live right. It seemed like the wicked people were always prospering. Why couldn't I prosper? If God was in control, why did I have to suffer? Some of you might be going through some difficult times and may be asking God the same questions right now. I struggled with these feelings and wrestled with God over them for about a year. I felt like a failure and that I had wasted wealth that I could never get back.

After a year of struggling with this, I finally realized that God knew he needed someone to take this message to hurting people. He knew I would be speaking to you through this book. He also knew you would not listen if I always had money and never had any huge amount of debt. He also knew I would have more compassion for others since God had shown compassion for me. It became so clear and simple. God allowed Carol and me to go through difficult financial times in order to give us this ministry. He allowed it because he loves us, and he allowed it for you.

I wrote *Financial Breakthrough* to share my personal story of being delivered from what seemed to be an unwinnable battle with debt. I have no doubt I was delivered from debt by God. This book explains how God delivered us from debt and how he will deliver you from your difficult financial situation. My prayer and hope is that my experiences in becoming debt-free and the biblical truths about money shared in this book will encourage you to begin your own journey to a financial breakthrough.

Introduction

I was watching football during the Thanksgiving weekend, and I couldn't help but notice the numerous commercials that encouraged the use of debt to make all my dreams come true. They promised, "No payments, no down payment, no interest for two years, and no annual fees." One company even advertised, "You are actually rewarded for using our card." We cannot blame the companies for marketing the use of credit because it makes great business sense. First, studies show that consumers are likely to spend 30%–40% more when using credit cards than when spending cash. In addition, most people who use credit cards carry a balance and therefore end up paying two to three times the amount of the original cost because of interest. Because they carry a balance month after month, consumers may end up paying $90 for a $30 shirt.

This book is not about berating companies for promoting the use of debt. In fact, I am employed by one of the fastest growing Visa credit card providers in America. This book is intended to help Christians better understand God's perspective on money and the use of debt.

Debt presumes on the future.

Although the Bible does not say using debt is a sin, it clearly discourages the use of debt. Debt presumes on the future. When we go into debt without a guaranteed way of repayment, we assume we will earn enough in the future to pay the debt. We are presuming that our jobs or income will continue. James 4:13–15 warns us against presuming on the future:

Now listen, you who say, "Today or tomorrow we will go to this or that city, spend a year there, carry on business and make money." Why, you do not even know what will happen tomorrow. What is your life? You are a mist that appears for a little while and then vanishes. Instead, you ought to say, "If it is the Lord's will, we will live and do this or that."

When we go into debt, we spend our future earnings today so that we are forever in a cycle of debt.

Debt is a form of slavery or bondage.

Debt affects many areas of life spiritually, mentally, and physically. Debt prevents us from building real wealth, and increases stress, which contributes to mental, physical, and emotional fatigue. In Proverbs 22:7, debt is described as a form of slavery or bondage:

The rich rule over the poor, and the borrower is servant to the lender.

One of Carol's favorite commercials is a Lending Tree commercial. A man comes on the screen and says, "I'm Stanley Johnson. I've got a great family. I've got a four-bedroom house in a great community. Like my car? It's new. I even belong to the local golf club. How do I do it? I'm in debt up to my eyeballs. I can barely pay my finance charges." The commercial finishes with Stanley pleading, "Somebody help me."

Today many of us live in financial chaos. Too often we are living paycheck to paycheck and using one credit card to pay the minimum on another credit card. To those around us we look like we really have it going on, but in reality, we are "in debt up to our eyeballs," and we have no real wealth. Although we have all the luxuries of life, we struggle to pay our bills, have no investments, and have no education fund for our children. We have improved our lifestyles through debt, only to discover the burden of debt then controls our lifestyle, and we become enslaved to our financial situation.

Financial freedom has little to do with how much money you earn. Financial freedom means being free of worries about how you will pay your bills, what will happen if you find yourself without a job for six months, or how you will take care of unforeseen emergencies. As a budget counselor, I have seen people who lack proper insurance for their family, yet their kids have $200 sneakers.

The average person in the United States has little or no money saved, regular obligations to support an excessive lifestyle, significant credit obligations, and a total dependence on next week's paycheck to stay afloat.

- According to The Motley Fool Credit Center, the average American carries $8,562 in credit card debt.

- *Jet Magazine* reports a study conducted by Citibank that 57% of all divorces are a result of financial tension in the home.

- More and more check-cashing companies charging over 300% in interest are popping up in low-income neighborhoods.

- Lenders are preying on those caught up in wanting it all now, which is leading to an increase in bankruptcies and foreclosed homes.

This book is intended to help those who may be trapped by their debt situation. We will discuss how debt affects our lives, what the Bible has to say about debt, specific steps you can take to get out of debt, and finally wealth-building tips for a life after debt. Thank you for taking this first step toward your financial breakthrough.

1

Why Should Christians Talk about Money?

How we handle money influences our fellowship with God.

Money is a difficult subject to teach in the Christian church. The minute you mention it people start to tense up. When the average churchgoer thinks about the Bible and money, the first thing that comes to mind is to give 10% to God as a tithe. Most Christians are not aware that the Bible has 2,359 verses on how to handle money and possessions. Jesus spoke more about money than almost any other subject. He did so for three reasons:

The first reason is that how we handle money influences our fellowship with God. In Luke 16:11, Jesus says:

For if you have not been faithful in the use of worldly wealth, who will entrust the true riches with you?

In this verse, Jesus equates how we handle money with how much God can trust us. Jesus is saying, "If you cannot handle money, then I cannot trust you. If you can handle money a little, I can trust you a little." In other words, handling money properly indicates spiritual maturity.

Money is God's primary competitor to be first in our lives.

The second reason is money is God's primary competitor to be first in our lives. Jesus tells us in Matthew 6:24:

We cannot serve two masters, either we hate one and love the other. You cannot serve both God and money.

When the Crusade was being fought during the twelfth century, the Crusaders hired mercenaries to fight for them. Because it was a religious war, the mercenaries were baptized before fighting. While being baptized, they would hold their sword out of the water to symbolize that Jesus was not in control of their swords. They would use their swords any way they pleased. That is how many of us treat God when it comes to our money. We say, "God you can control every other area of my life, but I'll take care of my money and spend it any way I please."

So much of our lives revolve around money that it becomes a target for Satan to get a stronghold in our lives.

The third reason Jesus talked about money is that so much of our lives revolves around money that it becomes a target for Satan to get a stronghold in our lives. Because we spend most of our lives earning, spending, taking care of, and thinking about our money and possessions, we create a vulnerable area for Satan to attack. In Matthew 4:8–10, Satan even tried to tempt Jesus this way:

Again, the devil took him to a very high mountain and showed him all the kingdoms of the world and their splendor. "All this I will give you," he said, "if you will bow down and worship me." Jesus said to him, "Away from me, Satan! For it is written: 'Worship the Lord your God, and serve him only.'"

If he tried attacking Jesus with money, don't you think Satan will try attacking you that way? If Satan were tempting Jesus today, he might say, "You can have all the possessions in the world—that big house, a brand new Mercedes and Hummer, a lot of bling-bling, a country club membership, dining at all the fanciest places, a plasma TV—all of it if you bow down and worship me." Jesus would respond, "Never. I will worship the Lord God and serve him only." Now you may say, "Well, that's not me. I worship God not money," but the Bible tells us that when you borrow, you are servant to the lender. God wants you to be his servant only. In John 10:10 Jesus said,

"I have come that they may have life, and have it to the full."

Jesus talked about money because he wanted to give us a road map for living without financial worries.

2

Why Did I Get into Debt in the First Place?

There are four common causes of problem debt.

Ron Blue, a noted Christian financial counselor, believes there are four common causes of problem debt: a lack of discipline, a lack of contentment, a search for security, and a search for significance.

Because the problems overlap somewhat, you probably see yourself in more than one category. Debt does not discriminate. These four causes are shared by everyone, regardless of race, class, or religion.

Discipline

Most people fall into debt because of a lack of discipline. People who lack discipline do not realize they are overspending. They are just going through life carelessly spending, until one day they look up, and they are seriously in debt. They wonder, "How can that be? I don't live lavishly. I make good money. Why don't I ever seem to have enough money to pay my bills?" The thought of a budget terrifies these people. Some of us are naturally more disciplined than others because of our personalities, and some learn to be disciplined over time. Some of us are disciplined in some aspect of our lives but not in other areas. If you are not naturally self-disciplined, do not worry because it is a skill that can be acquired.

Discipline is making the right decision consistently.

Galatians 5:22–23 lists discipline or self-control as a fruit of the Spirit:

But the fruit of the Spirit is love, joy, peace, patience, kindness, goodness, faithfulness, gentleness, and [discipline].

The more you allow God to operate in your life, the more disciplined you will become. In his book *The Debt Squeeze,* Blue defines discipline as "making the right decision consistently." I was up early one morning praying, and God revealed to me some truths I need to incorporate into my life:

- Choose to be disciplined.
- Allow God to fill me with his power to be disciplined.
- Make a plan to be disciplined.

You can become more disciplined by spending time with God, praying and meditating, talking with him about your weakness, trusting him to help you, and being attentive to God's plan. This requires something that is foreign to many of us—quiet time. During this quiet time, list the thoughts God reveals to you. Write them down so they are clear, and commit to this plan immediately. This book will help you in the process, but ultimately being disciplined is a choice that only you can make.

Contentment

Being content does not mean that we never want the best God has to offer, but it does mean we depend on God to provide it.

Many times, we rationalize going into debt because we are not content with what we have. In fact, we often envy or covet what others have. Paul writes in Philippians 4:11–13:

...for I have learned to be content whatever the circumstances. I know what it is to be in need, and I know what it is to have plenty. I have learned the secret of being content in any and every situation, whether well fed or hungry, whether living in plenty or in want. I can do everything through him who gives me strength.

Being content does not mean that we never want the best God has to offer, but it does mean we depend on God to provide it.

Recently, my wife and I struggled with a decision to replace her minivan. We have six in our family, so for us to transport everyone we need at least a six-passenger vehicle. We currently have no car payments. Her minivan is 10 years old, has 150,000 miles, and is starting to have the cosmetic wear and tear of being a family vehicle for four kids. Overall, the car has few mechanical problems and runs fine.

Because I know nothing about cars, I spent months researching the best replacement vehicle. I came up with vehicle choices based on economics, reliability, and meeting our needs. Carol, on the other hand, said she wanted a car that looks good. We settled on a used, low-mileage, seven-passenger vehicle that Carol liked. We had enough money in our retirement and children's education funds to pay cash, but we both knew that taking money from those accounts to pay for a car was not a good decision. Since we did not have enough cash on hand to pay for the vehicle, we looked at our budget to see if we could afford financing the vehicle. We realized we had an extra several hundred dollars a month by making a few minor adjustments. Therefore, we determined we could finance the vehicle.

We started shopping around at local dealers, in the newspaper, and on the Internet for this particular vehicle. We found one that fit our criteria at a great price on the Internet. Before making a major purchase, I had to check the advice of my Christian accountability partners. I walked through the decision with them, and they agreed it seemed like a good decision. Just before making an offer, I said a little prayer. "God, I think this is a good decision, but if this is not your will for me then let me know, and I'll stop right now."

I felt at peace with the decision, so I made an offer and received an e-mail that the seller had accepted it. It was a great car at a great price. I called the seller to arrange to pick it up, and I was told, "I'm sorry, but I sold that vehicle to someone else." I could not believe it. Initially, I was mad. "What do you mean you sold my car?" Then I remembered my prayer and realized God had other plans. I started my search again. I also kept praying to God about it, but God just would not release me to buy a car. Instead, he was encouraging me to be content with what we had until he provided more. God revealed that he wanted me to put the money in a car savings account each month so when the time arrived, I would have the cash available to purchase the car, or at least to make a down payment to lower our monthly payments. There was no doubt that God would provide us the vehicle we desired at the right time. Our job is to be content with what we have and be disciplined about our savings until he changes our situation.

The problem many of us have is that we want everything now. That is what advertisers are marketing to us. "Why wait when you can have it now?" Advertisements are intended to make you discontented with what you have. You thought your thirty-six inch TV was great until you saw a fifty-inch, high-definition, wall-mounted plasma TV advertised in the paper.

My brother told me a story about one of his tenants. As he went to collect the rent that was a couple of months late, he noticed the tenant had recently purchased a sixty-inch big-screen TV. The tenant talked about how they wished they could afford to own a home, but that they were having trouble paying the rent. My brother asked why they would purchase a sixty-inch TV for an eight hundred square-foot house, when their goal was to one day own their own home. The tenant rationalized that they were getting the TV now so they would have it when they moved into the home. Sadly, this is how many of us think. Our desire to have it now sabotages our ability to reach our goals in the future.

Discontentment causes us to spend our future earnings today so we are forever in a cycle of debt. Contentment is not something we are born with. Paul's statement, "I have learned to be content," suggests that contentment is something we all have to learn. It can only be learned through spiritual maturity and applying the biblical principles God provides in scriptures.

Security

As Christians, our security comes from a personal relationship with Jesus Christ.

A need for security drives many people to overspend. It amazes me how we get married or begin our careers and try to start right now with everything it took our parents twenty years to get. We want a new fully furnished house, a new car, fancy clothes, and lavish vacations. Moreover, we want it all now. Having these things might symbolize to the world a secure life, but Jesus warns against this in Matthew 6:19–21:

Do not store up for yourselves treasures on earth, where moth and rust destroy, and where thieves break in and steal. But store up for yourselves treasures in heaven, where moth and rust do not destroy, and where thieves do not break in and steal. For where your treasure is, there your heart will be also.

As Christians, our security comes from a personal relationship with Jesus Christ. Knowing we have security in Christ takes away the need to acquire things and allows us to be content with our circumstances. Once we place our security in Christ, we no longer have to spend money we do not have in order to feel secure, and we soon realize that acquiring more things could never fill our need for security.

Significance

Psalms 37:3–5:

Trust in the Lord, and do good; so shalt thou dwell in the land, and verily thou shalt be fed.

Delight thyself also in the Lord; and he shall give thee the desires of thine heart.

Commit thy way unto the Lord; trust also in him; and he shall bring it to pass.

Finally, some people go into debt because they are searching for significance. Acquiring certain things makes us feel better about ourselves. According to society, the most significant person is the one with the biggest home, the most expensive car, and the best toys. The more stuff we acquire, the more significant we are. Although we rarely admit it, we find that none of these things satisfies us. We say to ourselves, "If I only had more money, that new car, or that job, I would be happy." However, if we could find joy and peace in these things, why are so many rich and famous people unhappy? Many people who seem to have everything are sad, lonely, and searching for something that can provide them joy and peace.

Solomon was a biblical character who had it all. He had more wisdom, wealth, and riches than anyone living in his day. Despite having all the riches, he wrote in Ecclesiastes that life is meaningless without a personal relationship with God.

Just as Solomon did, we have to realize that significance comes only from God. We are significant because God made us in his own image. If God is significant, then so are we. One way God provides us significance is through loving relationships. It does not matter who you are or what you have done, you are still significant to someone who loves you. The worst parents still have some significance to their children. The worst prisoners on death row have someone who feels that their lives are significant. We are significant because God created us with unique skills, abilities, and desires in order to achieve a distinct purpose in life. Buying more stuff can never fulfill that need to be significant. Again, it is only when we have a relationship with God that we begin to realize we are significant and our lives have meaning. Realizing our significance allows us to put our money and possessions into perspective.

To Husbands and Wives

Generally speaking, husbands are less concerned about security than wives are. Wives desire a peaceful home free of worries about how bills will be paid and how she will provide for the kids. She wants to choose whether to work or stay at home to raise her kids. Men are more prone to overspending because of their need to feel significant. For us men, the more stuff we have means the more of a man we are. The best man has the biggest home, the most expensive car, and the fanciest toys. We proudly chant, "You da man," every time one of us tops another in any of these areas. Because security is not a primary concern, men often will leverage everything to fulfill their need for significance. Husbands should not frustrate their wives by threatening their need for security. Do not put your home or family at risk in order to feel significant, and be sure that your wife clearly understands and agrees to any financial decision you make.

Wives should not frustrate their husbands by creating debt. A man feels like a man when he can provide for his family and achieve God's great purpose for him. Your husband may have a plan that requires you to curtail spending today in order to accomplish bigger purposes in the future. Consistently overspending and creating debt only frustrates him and drives the two of you further apart. The key for couples is to balance the man's need for significance with the woman's need for security. The two of you must become partners in determining how you will handle money. You both have to spend time with God and lean on him to reveal his perfect will for your lives.

3

Our Role vs. God's Role

Before I provide practical steps in obtaining financial freedom, it is important to explain the different roles involved. We have a part, and God has a part. Many of us are confused about our part and God's part. God's part is summed up in 1 Chronicles 29: 11–12:

Everything in the heaven and earth is yours, O Lord, and this is your kingdom. We adore you as being in control of everything. Riches and honor come from you alone and you are the Ruler of all mankind; your hand controls power and might and it is at your discretion that men are made great and given strength. (Living Bible)

God's First Role Is Ownership

When we acknowledge God's ownership, every spending decision becomes a spiritual decision. We stop asking, "Lord, what should I do with <u>my</u> money?" Our question becomes, "Lord, what should I do with <u>your</u> money?"

God owns everything. The money we earn, the car we drive, and the home we live in are all his. We believe we own our money and possessions. As Christians, we are taught to give 10% to God and the rest is ours. However, that is not true. One hundred percent of it is God's. He created it all and never transferred ownership to people.

When we acknowledge God's ownership, every spending decision becomes a spiritual decision. We stop asking, "Lord, what should I do with *my* money?" Our question becomes, "Lord, what should I do with *your* money?" When you believe you own a particular possession, then the circumstances surrounding that possession will affect your attitude. If it is a favorable situation, then you are happy. Conversely, if it is unfavorable, you will be unhappy. In his book *Your Money Counts*, Howard Dayton shares a story about his friend Jim who had come to grips with the idea of God's ownership and then bought a new car. He had driven it only a few days when someone rammed into the side of it. Jim's first response was, "Lord, I don't know why you want a dent in your car, but now you've sure got a big one." Jim recognized God's ownership.

Trusting God with our possessions was a big step for me, especially concerning our home and car. At the time, we were going through debt issues, our house and car both needed some significant repairs. The roof was leaking, the carpet had stains, and the minivan had some mechanical issues. Trusting God meant I had to ask him what repairs I should make and how he wanted me to maintain his possessions. Consistently recognizing God's ownership is difficult, but if we are to have financial freedom, we must change our thinking about money and material things and recognize that it all belongs to God.

God's Second Role Is Control

To have the right attitude about money, we have to understand that God is in control. This is sometimes hard for us to grasp, especially when God allows difficult times. I shared our story of experiencing financial difficulties in the Preface. Realizing God is in control provided me peace that I was exactly where God needed me to be and gave me hope that God would change my situation. When discussing God's control, it is important to understand three reasons why God allows difficult times.

1. God allows difficult times to accomplish his intentions

The first reason God allows difficult times is to accomplish his intentions. You probably remember the story of Joseph. Joseph's brothers sold him into slavery because they were jealous of him. Although Joseph was thrown into prison, God did not allow him to stay there. He was promoted out of prison and eventually became the administrative head of Egypt, second only to Pharaoh. A famine hit the land where Joseph's family lived, and his family had to travel to Egypt to get food. Imagine what his brothers thought when they found out Joseph, whom they had tried to kill, now had the power to determine whether they lived or died. Many of us would have responded with revenge, but in Genesis 50:20, Joseph responded correctly by saying,

"Don't worry. It was not you who sent me here but God. What you meant for my bad, God meant for good. God sent me here to preserve my family."

Like Joseph, sometimes we go through difficult times so God can accomplish some bigger purpose in our lives. He did not make Joseph's brothers do what they did, and it does not take away from their wrongdoing. Nevertheless, God can take our bad situations and turn them around to accomplish his greater intentions.

Most people who know me know that I am a big Georgia Tech football fan. I went there on a football scholarship and became the starting nose guard my red-shirt freshmen year. At that time, I thought, like most other players, that I would go on to play professional football. I injured my knee, and little by little, my physical abilities deteriorated until I was no longer able to play. I lost my scholarship and flunked out of school. Things were not looking pretty, but God had other plans. What looked like a terrible situation turned out to be one of the best experiences of my life. I begged school officials to let me back into school before my parents discovered my situation. Fortunately, the school officials granted my request. Because I lost my scholarship, I began working to pay for school. I gained vital experience by working closely with Andrew Young and Maynard Jackson as they campaigned for governor of Georgia and mayor of Atlanta, respectively. I also built lasting friendships that I still cherish to this day. In my senior year, I received the most desired honor for a Georgia Tech graduate when I was selected to Tech's most prestigious honors organization. Nine months before graduation, I had accepted an offer to begin my career as an engineer with a Fortune 500 company. I am convinced none of that would have happened if I had not been injured in football. In this situation, I learned, as Joseph did, that God can turn what looks like a bad deal into something positive.

2. God allows difficult times for character development

The second reason God allows difficult times is to develop our character. In Romans 5:3–4, Paul writes:

Not only so, but we also rejoice in our sufferings, because we know that suffering produces perseverance; perseverance, character; and character, hope.

Your character is the real you that comes out when no one else is watching. It determines whether you will do the right thing even if no one else will know about it. Paul reminds us that our difficult times draw us closer to God. Rick Warren writes in *Celebrate Recovery,* "People are ready to take the first step to recovery when their pain is greater than their fear." When you have suffered enough and realize you can only turn to God to get you out of your mess, you are ready for him to build your character. It is easy to say you have faith when times are good, but it is when you are guaranteed to fail if God does not show up that you really build character and faith. The bigger the mess he pulls you out of, the more you grow in character. God knows he can trust me now with money. You cannot convince me that God cannot deliver me in a time of need. God will use difficult times to build your character, too.

3. God allows difficult times for discipline

Hebrews 12:6 states:

The Lord disciplines those he loves.

The third reason God allows difficult times is to discipline his children. Just as we discipline our kids to teach them right from wrong, God does the same with us. He allows us to feel the result of our poor decisions so we know not to go down that road. Some of us do not believe the fire is hot unless we touch it. Therefore, in some cases, God uses the tough times to teach us a lesson. Carol and I learned so many vital lessons about how God wants us to handle money. We have become very disciplined in our spending, saving, and giving. I believe because we have learned these lessons, God can freely bless us financially knowing he can trust us with money.

God's Third Role Is Provider

Matthew 6:25–33:

"Therefore I tell you, do not worry about your life, what you will eat or drink; or about your body, what you will wear. Is not life more important than food, and the body more important than clothes? Look at the birds of the air; they do not sow or reap or store away in barns, and yet your heavenly Father feeds them. Are you not much more valuable than they? Who of you by worrying can add a single hour to his life?

"And why do you worry about clothes? See how the lilies of the field grow. They do not labor or spin. Yet I tell you that not even Solomon in all his splendor was dressed like one of these. If that is how God clothes the grass of the field, which is here today and tomorrow is thrown into the fire, will he not much more clothe you, O you of little faith? So do not worry, saying, 'What shall we eat?' or 'What shall we drink?' or 'What shall we wear?' For the pagans run after all these things, and your heavenly

Father knows that you need them. But seek first his kingdom and his righteousness, and all these things will be given to you as well."

Jesus promises us he will provide for our basic needs. God cherishes this role. He compares it to that of any parent. Do your kids have to worry about their basic needs being provided? Who would have food or clothes and not give any to your children? Even the worst parents would not withhold food from their kids, so why would God? Because God owns everything, God is able and willing to provide all your needs.

There is a misunderstanding about God's promises concerning our needs verses our wants. Some Christian leaders teach that if we tithe then God will give us everything we want. They often provide scripture that seems to support that God promises us all our wants. For example, Psalm 37:4 says, *"Delight yourself in the Lord and he will give you the desires of your heart."* This verse and others reveal God's delight in providing special blessings to his faithful children, but God never promised us that he would give us everything we want every time.

God wants to bless us and enjoys blessing us, but he also knows what is best for us and will only provide our wants that align with his will for us.

We have four children. How would it look if we gave them everything they asked for or if we allowed them to do everything they wanted to do? We all know that would be foolish. As parents, we know what is best for them, and we do what is best so that they grow up healthy and well balanced. As our heavenly father and provider, God does the same for us. God wants to bless us and enjoys blessing us, but he also knows what is best for us and will only provide our wants that align with his will for us.

Even during that difficult financial period for us, God kept his promise to provide for us. We enrolled in a Crown Financial small group class offered at Bellevue Baptist Church in Memphis, Tennessee. This class was a twelve-week, in-depth study of what scripture teaches about money and possessions. This is where we learned many of the principles that are discussed in this book. Through Crown Financial, we were able to enter into a closer relationship with Jesus Christ as we learned to apply his word to our financial situation. We left Crown still in debt but with a clear plan on steps we needed to take to move toward financial freedom.

In 2002, things started to turn around. We stopped using credit cards and finally had a balanced budget, which means we were spending less than we earn. Nevertheless, we still had a lot of debt. We were paying $1,160 a month in finance charges alone and were only able to pay about $50 a month against the principle. I remember Carol saying, "Travis, at this rate it's going to take us forever to get out of debt." I responded, "That's not our part. Our part is to be diligent about our spending and trusting God to do his part."

It was not the elimination of our debt that gave us financial peace. We received peace the minute we turned our financial situation over to God and started helping others.

In 2002, we started teaching Crown Financial small groups at our home church, New Direction Christian Church, also in Memphis. It may seem odd that we began teaching even though we were still in debt, but this was a critical step in God's plan to bring peace into our finances. It was not the elimination of our debt that gave us financial peace. We received peace the minute we turned our financial situation over to God and started helping others. I remember when I taught my first class and realized this was why God allowed me to go through debt. I was so overwhelmed with God's presence. I told God, "If I have to stay in debt in order to be in your will and to experience this closeness with you, then I'm OK with having this debt the rest of my life." Honestly, I was at peace. I was at a place Bruce Wilkerson calls "sanctuary" in his book *The Dream Giver*. I felt God, and I just wanted to be where he was and in his perfect will. I had completely turned my financial troubles over to him.

Even though I was OK with being where I was, I am so glad God was not satisfied with me being in debt. He just had to get me to the point where I chose his way instead of the world's way. I am honored to report that by 2005, God had eliminated all of our debt except our mortgage. We paid off our car loan, funded our children's education, supported various ministries, and endowed a scholarship fund for my high school. God wants to bless you as well. His only requirement is that you allow him to be first in your life. God is like the horses at the Kentucky Derby waiting at the starting block. He cannot wait until that gate comes up. He is anxiously waiting for you to raise the starting gate by doing your part and allowing him to come in as Lord of your life.

Our Role Is Good Stewardship

Genesis 1:26:

Then God said, "Let us make man in our image, in our likeness, and let them rule over the fish of the sea and the birds of the air, over the livestock, over all the earth, and over all the creatures that move along the ground."

God made us to have authority over the world. We are stewards over all God created. A steward or manager is someone who has responsibility to take care of something that belongs to another. The Parable of the Talents in Matthew 25:14–30 is a great example of stewardship.

"Again, it will be like a man going on a journey, who called his servants and entrusted his property to them. To one he gave five talents of money, to another two talents, and to another one talent, each according to his ability. Then he went on his journey. The man who had received the five talents went at once and put his money to work and gained five more. So also, the one with the two talents gained two more. But the man who had received the one talent went off, dug a hole in the ground and hid his master's money.

"After a long time the master of those servants returned and settled accounts with them. The man who had received the five talents brought the other five. 'Master,' he said, 'you entrusted me with five talents. See, I have gained five more.'

"His master replied, 'Well done, good and faithful servant! You have been faithful with a few things; I will put you in charge of many things. Come and share your master's happiness!'

"The man with the two talents also came. 'Master,' he said, 'you entrusted me with two talents; see, I have gained two more.'

²³*"His master replied, 'Well done, good and faithful servant! You have been faithful with a few things; I will put you in charge of many things. Come and share your master's happiness!'*

"Then the man who had received the one talent came. 'Master,' he said, 'I knew that you are a hard man, harvesting where you have not sown and gathering where you have not scattered seed. So I was afraid and went out and hid your talent in the ground. See, here is what belongs to you.'

"His master replied, 'You wicked, lazy servant! So you knew that I harvest where I have not sown and gather where I have not scattered seed? Well then, you should have put my money on deposit with the bankers, so that when I returned I would have received it back with interest.'

"Take the talent from him and give it to the one who has the ten talents. For everyone who has will be given more, and he will have an abundance. Whoever does not have, even what he has will be taken from him. And throw that worthless servant outside, into the darkness, where there will be weeping and gnashing of teeth."

This scripture shows that as stewards, we have a responsibility to invest money wisely. It also illustrates that God does not provide us all with the same resources or potential. Neither does he expect us all to accumulate the same wealth. Because God is all-knowing and he provides as he sees fit, we have no reason to envy or covet what others have. It pleases God when we take what we have and multiply it. God wants us to be productive. Luke 16:12 tells us that it is only when we can be faithful with the little things that God can trust us with more. One day we all will come face to face with God, and he will hold us accountable for our actions. On that day, I want to hear God say, "Well done, my good and faithful servant." This desire keeps me committed to being a faithful steward.

4

Is It Faith or Are We Tempting God?

Matthew 4:5–7:

Then the devil took him to the holy city and had him stand on the highest point of the temple. "If you are the Son of God," he said, "throw yourself down. For it is written:

"He will command his angels concerning you, and they will lift you up in their hands, so that you will not strike your foot against a stone."

Jesus answered him, "It is also written: 'Do not put the Lord your God to the test.'"

In the verses above, Satan tempted Jesus, "If you are the Son of God, throw yourself down." Satan tries to use our faith against us. We see this often today. Any good salesperson who recognizes a Christian will tell him to "step out on faith" that they can make the payments or "the ability to use credit is a blessing from God." Unfortunately, we often perpetuate this fallacy as Christians. I often hear quotations like "name it and claim it" or "you deserve the best" taken out of context. Although it is true that God wants to provide for his children, as Christians we must learn the difference between having faith and tempting God.

Jesus responded, "It is also written: 'Do not put the Lord your God to the test.'" We know God could have saved Jesus if he had jumped off the cliff. That is often how the devil works. He mixes just enough truth in with lies to make us believe it. Nevertheless, Jesus understood the difference between having faith and tempting God.

Satan attempts the same trick when it comes to our finances. "Go ahead, and buy that car. Don't you have faith that God will provide? It all belongs to God, and he wants the best for you. Your neighbor has one, and he is not even a Christian.

Don't you think God would want you to have it? Why wait until you have cash? You can get it on easy monthly payments. So what if it will take you seven years to pay it off? You deserve it."

It does not take faith to get something on credit. Credit allows us to see and touch what we want now rather than waiting on God to deliver it.

We are deceived into going deep into debt believing we are stepping out on faith. A good friend shared this analogy with me. Many of us have airbags in our cars. What if I took you for a ride in my car and started driving recklessly, speeding at 100 mph and avoiding any red lights or stop signs? When you ask me to be careful, I reply, "Don't worry, I have airbags." That is exactly what we are doing when we spend money we do not have and expect God to save us. Yes, God can save us, but this is not how he wants us to live. God wants us to live in peace.

Debt is damaging because it opposes the concept of delayed gratification. Delayed gratification means we are rewarded in the future for actions taken today. This is one of the foundations of faith. Hebrews 11:1 says, "Now faith is being sure of what we hope for and certain of what we do not see." It does not take faith to get something on credit. Credit allows us to see and touch what we want now rather than waiting on God to deliver it. Using credit requires no faith at all. In fact, debt allows us to play God and play right into Satan's trap.

Satan does not want you to practice delayed gratification because it matures you as Christians. If you can save your money until you have enough to pay cash, then how easy is it for you to do good work for Christ and trust him to reward you in heaven? When we follow this concept, we are practicing faith. Even when our situation looks impossible, we continue doing our part, and trust God to do his part.

5

Ten Steps to a Financial Breakthrough

In this chapter, I recommend practical steps you should take to get out of a problem debt situation. My wife and I know these steps work, because this is the path we took in getting out of debt. It is important that you wholeheartedly follow all the steps. The journey to becoming debt-free will require faith, hope, and discipline, but be encouraged that God will help you through it. Let's continue your journey to a financial breakthrough.

Step 1—Turn your situation over to God.

2 Kings 4:1–7:

The wife of a man from the company of the prophets cried out to Elisha, "Your servant my husband is dead, and you know that he revered the Lord. But now his creditor is coming to take my two boys as his slaves."

Elisha replied to her, "How can I help you? Tell me, what do you have in your house?" "Your servant has nothing there at all," she said, "except a little oil."

Elisha said, "Go around and ask all your neighbors for empty jars. Don't ask for just a few. Then go inside and shut the door behind you and your sons. Pour oil into all the jars, and as each is filled, put it to one side."

She left him and afterward shut the door behind her and her sons. They brought the jars to her and she kept pouring. When all the jars were full, she said to her son, "Bring me another one." But he replied, "There is not a jar left." Then the oil stopped flowing.

She went and told the man of God, and he said, "Go, sell the oil and pay your debts. You and your sons can live on what is left."

In this passage, a widow was threatened with losing everything she had to her creditors, and she appealed to Elisha for help. God multiplied what little she had to be more than enough to repay her debts. Carol and I experienced the same miraculous power of God to get us out of debt.

It is human nature for us to limit God's power by looking at our situation as the world does. For instance, Carol and I could only afford to pay $50 a month against our debt. It does not take a genius to know $50 a month for three years does not equal $100,000 of debt repayment. What we fail to understand is that God does not operate in terms of addition but in terms of multiplication. God took our little effort and multiplied it with his power. It is impossible for me to explain how this happens, but we are living proof that it is true.

God provided many miracles toward us becoming debt-free, but none was bigger than a six-month period beginning in November 2003.

In November 2003, God revealed that I would experience a career change. Through my daily scripture reading and meditation, God instructed me to trust him and to be attentive to his word. God gave me two scriptures during my meditation:

Proverbs 3:5–6:

Trust in the Lord with all your heart
and lean not on your own understanding;

in all your ways acknowledge him,
and he will make your paths straight.

And Romans 8:28:

And we know that in all things God works for the good of those who love him, who have been called according to his purpose.

I was not sure what the change would be, but I was excited to know that God was about to bless me with a new career opportunity. A couple of weeks later, I was shocked to find myself without a job. Although I was surprised and unsure what my next step would be, I was at peace with my situation. I was determined to trust God. I felt that God did not want me to rush out to look for a new job. I was confident that God would provide me with the right job and would provide for my family in the meantime. I spent the next several months enjoying time with my family, spending prayer time with God, and being attentive to his guidance. I only pursued career opportunities in which I felt God's direction.

During this time, we never experienced financial stress. We never went hungry, our kids continued their activities, and every bill was paid on time. By this time, Carol and I were committed to no new debt, so we were not going to use credit cards, even if it meant we would lose our home. As God's miracles would have it, our situation never came to that. Just like the widow in 2 Kings, money never ran out. God provided money from somewhere every time we needed it. The key was that we had fully turned over our situation to God. After six months without work, God opened a door to a new and exciting job opportunity. Not only had God provided for my family during my time without a job, but he also blessed us to eliminate all of our debt by the end of the year.

God only performs miracles when the challenge in front of us is so large that there is no way we can do it by our own power. If we could do it ourselves, then we would not need God and he would not get the glory. There was no way Carol and I could have gotten out of $100,000 in debt in three years by our own power. It had to come from God. God receives all the praise and glory from delivering us from debt, and he wants to get glory out of your situation, too. Just as he did with us, God will multiply your efforts to eliminate debt if you remain faithful. God is just waiting for you to do your part by following the direction laid out in his word and then turn it all over to him to provide his blessing.

Step 2—List everything you own and everyone you owe.

Use the blank financial statement (**Appendix A**) and debt list (**Appendix C**) to list everything you own and everyone you owe. Our initial financial statement (**Appendix B**) and debt list (**Appendix D**) are provided as examples. Believe me, it was hard for us to view on paper how bad our situation really was. Even though Carol and I were the only ones to see it, I was embarrassed that I had allowed our finances to get this way. It seems most of us don't do this step because we are afraid to learn how much we really owe. We prefer to be in the dark when it comes to our finances. We think if we ignore it, maybe the debt will go away. However, in reality, it is critical to see the total picture...no matter how bad it looks. In 1 John 1:5–10, Paul warns us about this very thing:

This is the message we have heard from him and declare to you: God is light; in him there is no darkness at all. If we claim to have fellowship with him yet walk in the darkness, we lie and do not live by the truth. But if we walk in the light, as he is in the light, we have fellowship with one another, and the blood of Jesus, his Son, purifies us from all sin.

If we claim to be without sin, we deceive ourselves and the truth is not in us. If we confess our sins, he is faithful and just and will forgive us our sins and purify us from all unrighteousness. If we claim we have not sinned, we make him out to be a liar and his word has no place in our lives.

Paul prefaced this statement by saying in verse four, *"We write this to make {your} joy complete."* Paul knows that when we try to keep our little mess a secret, we allow Satan to come into our lives. Earlier I mentioned that the number one cause of divorce is financial difficulties. Many times, couples wait until it is too late to address their financial problems. Sometimes spouses even keep financial problems from each other. Oprah Winfrey did a show in the fall of 2005 about a wife who had kept a large sum of credit card debt a secret from her husband. The enemy may not be able to affect your relationship with God directly, but walking in the darkness allows Satan to affect your relationship with your spouse or others. The above scripture tells us that if we allow God to shine light on our situation, we will have fellowship with one another. Writing down everything you own and everyone you owe exposes your situation to yourself, your spouse, and symbolically to God. He already knows, but just as he did with Adam when he asked, "Where are you?", he wants you to expose your problems to him. This scripture reminds us that only then will he change our situation and only then can we move toward a financial breakthrough.

A secondary benefit of listing what you own is that it could highlight items you can sell to accelerate debt repayment or to reduce monthly expenses. For instance, if you own a third vehicle you only drive on special occasions, you could sell it to pay off other debt while reducing your cost of maintenance, vehicle taxes, and insurance.

Step 3—Establish a budget.

Luke 14:28:

Suppose one of you wants to build a tower. Will he not first sit down and estimate the cost to see if he has enough money to complete it?

Jesus reminds us that it is wise to start with a plan or budget before beginning to spend. A budget helps you plan how you will spend your money. You create a budget by first tracking your spending over a month to see where you spend money. Use **Appendix E** to track your spending. After tracking your spending for a month, list it in Column A of **Appendix G**. Calculate your suggested spending using the suggested spending percentages in **Appendix F**. List suggested spending in Column B of **Appendix G**. Use the information in **Appendix G** to identify areas that you can reduce spending. A completed worksheet is provided in **Appendix H** as a sample.

Most of us spend more than we make, which results in a budget deficit. There are only two ways to balance a budget: make more money or spend less money. Most of the time, our earnings are sufficient. The problem occurs in our spending habits. You might be amazed at how we spend our hard-earned money on what we consider insignificant things. For instance, a person who stops at Starbucks to get their daily cup of coffee and an occasional muffin may be surprised that they are spending $140 a month on this small habit. David Bach calls this the "latte factor" in his book *The Automatic Millionaire.*

Look for ways to reduce your spending. Small adjustments can make a huge difference in achieving financial freedom. Some of the small changes we made included eliminating cable television, reducing options on our phone such as call waiting, caller ID, and long distance, and brown-bagging my lunch instead of eating out.

Many people fail at budgeting because it becomes cumbersome to keep up with receipts and track expenses daily. Families that simplify the money-handling process are more likely to remain within their budget. There are several useful tips to simplify budgeting that we use and recommend to others:

- Stop using credit and debit cards. We are likely to spend 30%–40% more when using a credit card than with cash.

- Maintain a balanced checkbook to minimize bank fees. Only write a check when you know you have cash in your account.

- Withdraw cash to use the "envelope system" for food, clothing, entertainment, and miscellaneous expenses. Stop spending when money runs out.

Step 4—Create a debt repayment plan.

Psalm 37:21:

The wicked borrow and do not repay, but the righteous give generously.

This scripture highlights that God intends for us to repay our debts. This does not mean you should not negotiate with your lenders. You should contact lenders to work out a repayment plan. In some cases, lenders will lower interest rates or settle your account with a smaller payoff. In many cases, you can negotiate with your lenders directly. If your debt is so high that this process overwhelms you, contact a reputable credit counseling service. Beware of those who advertise that they can fix your credit problems and make all of your debts go away. Although there are some reputable debt consolidators, the industry is full of scam artists trying to rip off trusting and hurting people. The only way to get out of debt is to repay your debts.

About this time you might be asking, "What about declaring bankruptcy?" Psalm 37:21, as well as other scriptures, supports that we should make every attempt to repay our debts. Crown Financial Ministries suggests, "Bankruptcy is permissible under two circumstances: a creditor forces a person into bankruptcy, or counselors believe the debtor's emotional health is at stake because of inability to cope with the pressures of creditors."

After developing your budget and determining how much you can pay each month against your debts, contact your lenders to work out the best repayment plan you can. You can only pay what you have, so do not get stressed out when you do not have enough to pay everything. If your creditors force you into bankruptcy, seek appropriate legal counseling. Nonetheless, you should make every reasonable attempt to negotiate a repayment before declaring bankruptcy.

Your monthly budget should include a reasonable amount to pay toward your debt. You may increase your monthly debt payment as you are able, but you should never decrease the amount over the repayment process. As you pay off one debt, you will take that amount and begin putting it toward the next debt. This is called the "snowball" effect and is recommended by many debt counselors. Before you begin paying off debts using the "snowball" effect, you must first identify which debts you should repay first.

List your debts from the lowest to the highest balance. Also, list the interest rates for each debt. Pay off your debts in the order of lowest to highest balance. Paying off smaller debts first will motivate you on your way to becoming debt-free. **Table 1** illustrates the order we used in repaying our debts.

Table 1: Debt Repayment Plan

Debtor	Min. Payment	Balance	Interest Rate
BOA Overdraft Credit	$18	$1,000	18.00%
Juniper Credit Card	$24	$1,000	12.00%
Wachovia	$0	$2,018	0.00%
Sallie Mae	$50	$4,500	5.00%
Universal Card	$103	$4,985	5.90%
Citi Bank*	$160	$7,741	12.90%
Chase	$142	$7,140	9.90%
Amex	$160	$8,000	10.90%
MBNA	$300	$18,968	17.99%
Wells Fargo	$203	$22,128	8.00%

*We put Citi Bank ahead of Chase because of the higher interest rate and balances were relatively close.

We paid $1,160 a month in debt repayments. After completely paying off BOA, we applied the $18 payment to the Juniper payment, making Juniper's payment $42 ($18 + $24). We continued moving down the list until all debts were repaid.

Step 5—Consider a radical change in lifestyle.

Selling our home made a significant impact on our ability to be debt–free. In 2001, we sold our 4,800-square-foot home and moved into a 3,100-square-foot home. This allowed us to reduce our budget by $1,000 a month. In 2004, a career change took us to Little Rock, Arkansas. At this time, our income continued to increase, and we were doing well financially. After prayerful consideration, Carol and I decided that if we downsized our home again, we could eliminate all nonmortgage debt. We moved into a great 2,100-square-foot home in a nice neighborhood. This change helped us reduce our mortgage and eliminate all other debt by the end of 2004. Prayerfully considering a radical change in lifestyle shows God that we are committed to doing whatever is necessary to be in his perfect will. Today, our monthly expenses are about half of our monthly income. This gives us a lot of flexibility in our savings, investing, and giving. Carol and I still feel that our adjustment in lifestyle is temporary. We believe God will provide a larger home for us one day, but until then, we have chosen to be content with our current home.

Step 6—Make a commitment to no new debt.

This step requires making a decision to be both disciplined and content. Committing to no new debt is our way of saying, "OK God, we are trusting you with our situation." It may mean you will have to perform "plastic surgery" on your credit cards to eliminate any temptation of using them. Be content with what you have until God provides more. As I mentioned earlier, Carol and I were tempted to finance a new car. Every day after work, I would check out the latest postings for this car on eBay. Every day, I became less and less content with our minivan. Finally, we made a commitment that we would save money in order to pay cash for our next car. Carol and I decided we would stop shopping on the Internet. If we had not done this, we certainly would have convinced ourselves to buy a car and finance it. I suggest you stop shopping, going to the mall, and looking through catalogs. You may even have to limit TV watching to avoid commercials. The less marketing and advertising you subject yourself to, the less temptation you will have to break your commitment to no new debt.

Step 7—Create an emergency fund.

One activity that is critical in this commitment to no new debt is to establish an emergency fund of at least $1,000. Emergency funds are there in case the car breaks down, the roof leaks, or you have a medical emergency. Remember that this fund is not intended for the new pair of shoes that you just have to have before the sale ends. My experience with emergency funds is that usage is very rare. If you use it more than once or twice a year, you may want to reconsider whether you are experiencing real emergencies.

A couple I recently counseled is a great example of the benefit of emergency funds. This couple had made significant improvement in their financial situation over only a few months. They went from considerably overspending their monthly budget to having a budget surplus and beginning their debt repayment plan. One change they made was creating an emergency fund.

I received a call from the husband one day, and he shared a recent event. The transmission on his wife's car needed major repair. They had accumulated $1,200 in their emergency fund, and the repairs would cost $900. He said a few months ago his attitude would have been, "Man, just when I get some money, something happens." Now he was praising God for providing the funds to take care of unplanned emergencies like this one. This couple was prepared for their little emergency because of their commitment to becoming more disciplined in their finances and to God's financial guidance.

Step 8—Seek godly financial counseling.

The Bible encourages us to seek counseling. Proverbs 19:20 says:

Listen to advice and accept instruction, and in the end you will be wise.

In addition, Proverbs 12:15 says:

The way of a fool seems right to him, but a wise man listens to advice.

Pride often keeps us from seeking good counsel. Seeking counsel is especially difficult for men. We do not want anyone telling us what to do. Often people who lose everything through financial troubles could have avoided the mistake if they had sought counseling from someone with a solid understanding of God's perspective concerning money.

Before making any major financial decisions, I seek advice from several sources. The first source is my wife. I have learned that God has given women a special intuition that men do not have. Carol does not have an MBA or experience in a variety of money matters. In fact, she struggles in handling money, but she has great insight into what is a good decision in regard to money. As I mentioned earlier, men should make sure their wives understand and agree to any financial decision they wish to make.

The second sources I use for counseling are my accountability partners. I have two people whom I seek advice from in making any major financial decisions. My accountability partners know everything about me. They know how much money I make, what investments I have, and how I spend money. I have made a commitment to not carry out any decision they do not agree with. You cannot have just anyone be your accountability partner. You have to choose someone who is mature spiritually and has a solid understanding of God's perspective concerning money. When there is no accountability, it is easy to talk yourself into or to be talked into making a wrong decision. Many salespeople count on this. Conversely, having to explain your decision to someone is a great deterrence from making a "dumb" decision.

You may also seek professional counseling from a certified Christian financial counselor. The counselor could be fee based or nonfee based, but in either case, he or she will not sell you financial products or services. This guarantees they have no ulterior motives in counseling you. You can find Christian financial counselors through Crown Financial Ministries (www.Crown.org) and Dave Ramsey's Financial Peace University (www.daveramsey.com). Both of these organizations offer various workshops and seminars that can get you off to a great start in experiencing financial freedom. Carol and I attended Crown Ministry as small-group participants when we were deep in debt. If we had not made that twelve-week commitment, I am certain we would not be debt-free today.

Step 9—Create a plan to use windfalls to accelerate debt repayment.

All of us have fantasized about what we would do if we won the lottery. We already know we would pay off all of our debts, buy our dream house, provide gifts for our friends and relatives, take a vacation around the world, and even give a little charitable gift to our church. Despite the unlikelihood of this happening, we are often faced with smaller fortunes that come our way, yet we fail to take advantage of them. Think about the tax refunds, overtime pay, cash gifts, payments from insurance or legal settlements, and annual bonuses from work. It is as though God is providing our million-dollar lottery payout one thousand dollars at a time. These unexpected bonuses are God's answers to your prayers and can be used to help you reach your financial goals faster. Instead, many of us either squander extra funds trying to upgrade our standard of living or allow these funds to be absorbed into everyday living and bills. Steve and Annette Economides, authors of the *HomeEconomiser* newsletter, suggest a proactive approach to dealing with unexpected bonuses.

If you have debt to pay off, consider allotting:

- 60% to your smallest debt
- 20% to savings (emergency savings to keep from using credit)
- 10% to charitable giving
- 10% to enjoy

If you are out of debt except for your house, try allotting:

- 30% to your mortgage principle
- 30% to savings (emergency funds or retirement savings)
- 20% to house projects
- 10% to charitable giving
- 10% to enjoy

Carol and I followed a similar strategy to accelerate our debt repayment. We prayed for God to perform miracles in our lives, and he did. We wrote a plan that included our financial goals, as well as our wish list of ways we would enjoy money. Time and time again God blessed us with bonuses, big tax returns, gifts from friends and family, and unexpected extra funds. After honoring God with 10%, we were diligent in using the majority of these funds to accomplish our debt-free goal. However, we also made sure we used some of the unexpected money to enjoy. We took family vacations, bought some of the "toys" on our wish list, and just had some fun.

Every spring, millions of Americans receive a tax return, only to go out and spend it all. A few months later, we wonder where the money went. The amount of the extra income will not matter if you do not have a plan to use it. The key is to be prepared to handle God's blessing when it comes your way. Decide to use any windfall that comes your way to help you become debt-free and to build wealth.

Step 10—Don't give up.

Galatians 6:9:

Let us not become weary in doing good, for at the proper time we will reap a harvest if we do not give up.

The last step is don't give up. Some of you may feel like there is no use in even trying. Every time you have tried to fix your situation, it has gotten worse. You feel condemned by your past mistakes. Jesus spent so much time and energy talking about money because he knew it would be your toughest battle. However, Jesus is inviting you to trust him with your finances. All he wants is a more intimate relationship with you. He wants to be first in your life and wants you to experience peace in your finances. I urge you to remain strong as you progress toward your financial breakthrough.

6

Life after Debt

So far, most of this book has involved avoiding and getting out of debt. Getting your debt under control is only the first step toward becoming financially free. Now we can focus on life after debt.

Investing

When we begin investing, we stop worrying about looking wealthy and start focusing on becoming wealthy.

When discussing investing, it is important to address one question that often comes up. Is money evil? The answer to this is no! Money is neutral. Money is neither good nor evil. Money provides means for our necessities, as well as things that bring us great joy. The true joy the Bible speaks of includes having financial freedom. In fact, what kind of life would it be if you were always broke and unsure about how you would make ends meet? Matthew 17:24–27 demonstrates that Jesus had financial freedom during his walk on earth:

After Jesus and his disciples arrived in Capernaum, the collectors of the two-drachma tax came to Peter and asked, "Doesn't your teacher pay the temple tax?"

"Yes, he does," he replied. When Peter came into the house, Jesus was the first to speak. "What do you think, Simon?" he asked. "From whom do the kings of the earth collect duty and taxes—from their own sons or from others?"

"From others," Peter answered. "Then the sons are exempt," Jesus said to him. "But so that we may not offend them, go to the lake and throw out your line. Take the first fish you catch; open its mouth and you will find a four-drachma coin. Take it and give it to them for my tax and yours."

Jesus never worried about how he would eat, live, or pay bills. He showed that we should not live with these worries either. He desires for us to have financial freedom. Contrary to many beliefs, financial freedom is not just making large sums of money. I have witnessed many people who are financially free and have never made more than $20,000 a year. Conversely, there are plenty of people who make over $200,000 a year and still have no financial freedom. It is not about how much you make, but about what you do with what you earn. When we begin investing, we stop worrying about looking wealthy and start focusing on becoming wealthy.

God wants us to prosper so he can get glory from our lives. Who wants to serve a God who does not provide good things for his people? People are not attracted to poverty. The more he blesses you, the bigger witness you become to others. Investing in order to build wealth allows us to be better witnesses for God. When we invest and save, we are in better positions to provide for our families, leave an inheritance for our children, own and operate businesses, and serve God without concern for how we will pay for basic needs.

The Bible condemns the misuse of or having the wrong attitude toward money. Desiring wealth and financial independence is fine, but 1 Timothy 6:9–10 warns us from desiring to be rich:

People who want to get rich fall into temptation and a trap and into many foolish and harmful desires that plunge men into ruin and destruction. For the love of money is a root of all kinds of evil. Some people, eager for money, have wandered from the faith and pierced themselves with many griefs.

The problem comes when we place our desire to build wealth before our desire to serve God. He wants to be first in our lives and will not settle for less.

Jesus further illustrates this in Luke 12:16–21:

And he told them this parable: "The ground of a certain rich man produced a good crop. He thought to himself, 'What shall I do? I have no place to store my crops.'

"Then he said, 'This is what I'll do. I will tear down my barns and build bigger ones, and there I will store all my grain and my goods.' And I'll say to myself, "You have plenty of good things laid up for many years. Take life easy; eat, drink and be merry."

"But God said to him, 'You fool! This very night your life will be demanded from you. Then who will get what you have prepared for yourself?'

"This is how it will be with anyone who stores up things for himself but is not rich toward God."

It is wise for us to invest a portion of our money. However, God does not want us to focus solely on increasing our wealth. The Bible does not teach a certain percent to save or invest, but I agree with several Christian and non-Christian financial experts who suggest saving 10%–15% of your monthly income. Crown Financial Ministry's fundamental principle is to spend less than you earn and invest the difference over a long period of time.

Saving and investment goals should be categorized as either short-term or long-term. Short-term goals should include emergency savings and savings for large purchases like a vacation or vehicle. Your first short-term goal should be to increase your emergency savings to three to six times your monthly expenses. Once your vehicle is paid off, continue to pay this amount into a savings account so you can purchase a reliable, almost-new car when the time comes.

Long-term savings should consist of retirement investments to eliminate dependency on your current income, savings to operate a business if you so choose, funds for children's education if you have kids, as well as other investments for long-term wealth building. Invest 10%–15% of your gross income in long-term investments.

The Bible encourages us to avoid risky investments (Ecclesiastes 5:13–15) and to diversify our investment over seven or eight investments (Ecclesiastes 11:2). There are many investment vehicles, but my purpose is not to recommend specific investments. You can choose from many investment resources. A couple good books that helped us better understand investment options were David Bach's *The Automatic Millionaire* and Suze Orman's *The 9 Steps to Financial Freedom.*

If your company offers a matching 401(k) program, you should take advantage of this investment tool. In most cases, the company provides matching contributions, offers various investment choices, and lowers tax liabilities. Again, I suggest you use other resources to help you figure out the best investment vehicles for you.

Insurance and Estate Planning

In order to help provide for your family, you should have adequate insurance coverage and estate planning. Use the worksheet in **Table 2** to determine how much life insurance you need. In most cases, a low-cost, term policy is the best solution for life insurance coverage, but please refer to the resources listed above to identify the best insurance for you.

If you die without a will, state officials will determine where your kids will live and how your assets will be distributed. Having a will helps ensure your children are properly cared for after you are gone. Wills are relatively easy to complete. Carol and I purchased Orman's *Ultimate Protection Portfolio* for less than $50. This package included easy-to-complete estate-planning material. It took less than an hour to fill in our information. We then visited our local bank to have it notarized free. It was a very simple process. If you have not done so, I suggest you complete this as soon as possible.

Table 2: Life Insurance Worksheet

Life Insurance Worksheet

Present annual income needs:
Subtract deceased person's needs:

Subtract other income available:
(Social Security, investments, retirement)

= Net annual income needed:

Net annual income needed, multiplied by
12.5 (assumes an 8% after-tax investment
return on insurance proceeds)

Lump sum needs:
Debts:
Education:
Other:
Total lump sum needs:

**Total life insurance needs: (net annual
income needed + lump sum needs)**

Lifestyle

Philippians 4:11–13:

I am not saying this because I am in need, for I have learned to be content whatever the circumstances. I know what it is to be in need, and I know what it is to have plenty. I have learned the secret of being content in any and every situation, whether well fed or hungry, whether living in plenty or in want. I can do everything through him who gives me strength.

Too many times, we spend money that we do not have trying to impress people we do not like. Instead of building wealth, we spend money trying to keep up with the Joneses not realizing the Joneses are up to their eyeballs in debt and leading you down the same path.

Many wealthy people live well below their means. That is how they became wealthy in the first place. *The Millionaire Next Door* describes the typical millionaire as a person who lives well below his or her means, wears inexpensive clothes, lives in the same home for over twenty years, and drives inexpensive American-made cars. You ask, "How could that be? Why wouldn't millionaires have the finest clothes, most expensive homes, and luxury cars?" It is simple. They became millionaires because they believe being wealthy is more important than looking wealthy.

Dave Ramsey, author of *Financial Peace*, provides these secrets to living in financial peace. "Avoid the lifestyle of the rich when you are not rich. The best things in life, including good {stuff}, come only at the expense of personal discipline. You must limit your style of living. You must figure out how much your actual income is and then proceed to live well below that mark."

Clearly, God intends for us to spend money wisely. Wise spending does not mean you only buy things that are basic needs. God wants you to enjoy life and things. In June 2005, I was overwhelmed with balancing yard work with many other activities. One day a boy in the neighborhood offered to mow my lawn for a small fee. I realized that spending money in this case would free up my time, allowing me to do more in ministry and spend more time with my family. Wealth should allow us to simplify and enjoy life, not make it more complicated.

We are always faced with how we should spend money. Should we buy a bigger house, a luxury car, or the latest technology? The key is to prayerfully submit our spending decision to God.

I recently counseled a friend whose family was relocating to another state. He was questioning how much he should spend on his next home. We started with a review of his financial situation. My friend had been very diligent with investing and controlling spending. He has no debt, earns a high income, gives freely to his local church, and lives well below his income. After prayerfully submitting his spending decision to God, he purchased a very nice and what most people would consider expensive new home. Months later, my friend has been very pleased with his decision. He has a mortgage payment that easily fits his budget and a home that he and his family are enjoying very much. Just like my friend, God wants us to freely enjoy possessions when we submit our spending decision to him.

Teaching Children about Money

Once Carol and I understood what the Bible said about money, we realized we had an obligation to teach our kids how to handle money. Even though I got into debt, I still feel like my parents did a good job teaching me about money. I was taught to tithe, avoid debt, reduce tax liabilities, invest money, and enjoy the rest. I had only myself to blame for my financial problems, but I am convinced I would have been worse off if they had not taught me some of these basic principles.

I have witnessed many parents sending the wrong message about money to their kids. We fail to realize that kids are watching our every move. When my dad was alive, I went with him to collect from one of his tenants. The tenant tried to explain why they did not have the rent. However, I could not help but notice her two-year-old son with diamond stud earrings, wearing the latest expensive athletic shoes, and playing the latest video game. I am sure my kids would like all the latest things. However, I think they also enjoy having a nice home and participating in extracurricular activities. We influence our kids if we do not answer the phone when bill collectors call, or if we have our kids lie and tell the bill collector we are not home. We also influence them when we are wasteful with money.

It is natural for parents to want to buy things for their kids, but we have to be careful what messages we are sending them. *The Millionaire Next Door* talks about how some millionaires' kids are not taught the same basic principles that their parents were taught to become wealthy. Instead, the millionaire parents provide their children everything in life. The result is that the kids never realize the same level of wealth as their parents.

It is our responsibility as parents to teach our children the proper attitude about money. This means teaching kids how to budget, teaching kids about giving, involving kids in spending decisions, requiring kids to participate in household chores, allowing kids to earn extra money, and modeling a proper attitude toward money.

Carol and I have decided to provide an allowance for our kids once they reach school age. The amount increases each year until they complete the seventh grade, when they will be expected to earn their own money. Each of the kids has his or her own list of household chores. We give them freedom to spend their money with some guidelines. They are first required to give 10 percent to church. The remaining money is split between savings and spending. We helped our twelve-year-old establish a bank account. Our nine-year-old and seven-year-old have banks that are separated into three categories: giving, spending, and saving. We have not begun teaching our four-year-old yet. Our goal is to have each of our kids managing his or her own finances with the exception of food and shelter by the time he or she is a senior in high school. Although our children still do not fully understand the concept of money, we are certain that the habits we are establishing now will help them greatly down the road.

Honesty

Leviticus 19:11–13:

"Do not steal.
"Do not lie.
"Do not deceive one another.

"Do not swear falsely by my name and so profane the name of your God. I am the Lord.

"Do not defraud your neighbor or rob him.
"Do not hold back the wages of a hired man overnight."

God requires us to be totally honest with others. If we want to be blessed with more, we have to deal with others honestly. We cannot cheat on our taxes or obtain illegal cable and expect God to bless us. Dishonesty stems from pride or greed. Dishonesty hurts our ability to witness to others. Non-Christians are discouraged when dealing with dishonest people who profess to know God. Many would rather deal with dishonest non-Christians. At least then they know to expect dishonesty. Proverbs 14:2 teaches us that you cannot practice dishonesty and still love God. If you love God, you will do those things that please him.

Honesty provides a platform for us to be a light to others and puts us in a position to be blessed by God.

7

Giving

Malachi 3:8–10:

"Will a man rob God? Yet you rob me.

"But you ask, 'How do we rob you?'

"In tithes and offerings. You are under a curse—the whole nation of you—because you are robbing me. Bring the whole tithe into the storehouse, that there may be food in my house. Test me in this," says the Lord Almighty, "and see if I will not throw open the floodgates of heaven and pour out so much blessing that you will not have room enough for it."

Most people are familiar with verses in the Bible that speak to tithing, such as this one. We know these verses because many of us hear them every week at church services across the country. It seems some ministers misuse scripture to pressure congregations into giving money to the church. This trend is disturbing. Churches should not beg for money each week. Giving is an act of worship and should be a time of reverence.

I am convinced that if churches focus on growing members spiritually, they will never again have to pressure their congregations to give money.

Giving allows the giver to worship God and to be more intimate with him. I am convinced that if churches focus on growing members spiritually, they will never again have to pressure their congregations to give money. We have been fortunate to be a part of churches that reflect God in the area of giving. Our church rarely mentions tithing. At the end of services, a minister might remind the congregation that drop boxes are at each exit, but tithing at this church is never a pressured situation. In spite of the lack of pressure to tithe, our church is growing and has plans to build in two new locations in central Arkansas. Our church is able to fund this growth because of a congregation of cheerful givers.

During his walk on earth, Jesus showed that he was an unselfish giver. Giving allows us to take on more of his character. By giving, we are able not only to meet the needs of others but also to position ourselves to receive more blessings from God. Jesus promises this very thing while teaching his disciples in Luke 18:18–30:

A certain ruler asked him, "Good teacher, what must I do to inherit eternal life?"

"Why do you call me good?" Jesus answered. "No one is good—except God alone. You know the commandments: 'Do not commit adultery, do not murder, do not steal, do not give false testimony, honor your father and mother.'"

"All these I have kept since I was a boy," he said. When Jesus heard this, he said to him, "You still lack one thing. Sell everything you have and give to the poor, and you will have treasure in heaven. Then come, follow me."

When he heard this, he became very sad, because he was a man of great wealth. Jesus looked at him and said, "How hard it is for the rich to enter the kingdom of God! Indeed, it is easier for a camel to go through the eye of a needle than for a rich man to enter the kingdom of God."

Those who heard this asked, "Who then can be saved?" Jesus replied, "What is impossible with men is possible with God." Peter said to him, "We have left all we had to follow you!"

"I tell you the truth," Jesus said to them, "no one who has left home or wife or brothers or parents or children for the sake of the kingdom of God will fail to receive many times as much in this age and, in the age to come, eternal life."

Jesus' words confirm that by being a cheerful giver we will be rewarded both in heaven and while on earth.

Jesus speaks of having the right attitude toward giving in Matthew 6:1–4:

"Be careful not to do your 'acts of righteousness' before men, to be seen by them. If you do, you will have no reward from your Father in heaven.

"So when you give to the needy, do not announce it with trumpets, as the hypocrites do in the synagogues and on the streets, to be honored by men. I tell you the truth, they

have received their reward in full. But when you give to the needy, do not let your left hand know what your right hand is doing, so that your giving may be in secret. Then your Father, who sees what is done in secret, will reward you."

Giving is a personal decision and should be done prayerfully, cheerfully, and without pride. For a long time I was very prideful about my giving. I felt good that I had a high income and was able to give a larger amount than others. Through my own financial difficulties, God dealt with me on my prideful attitude. I no longer look for opportunities to draw attention to my giving. In fact, we currently send our tithes to our local church automatically from our checking every payday.

As we grow in our area of giving, God continues to bless us financially so we can be even more of a blessing to others.

Giving to Our Local Church

God directs us to give to our local churches. Some people have problems with giving money to churches because they fear the ministers are just getting rich. Some even feel like people in ministry should be poor, but that view is not scriptural. It pains me to see those who pastor churches with hundreds of members and yet are required to work full time to make ends meet. 1 Timothy 5:17 says:

The elders who direct the affairs of the church well are worthy of double honor, especially those whose work is preaching and teaching.

Ministry is hard work. Ministers provide us great service with their teachings, prayers, encouragement, guidance, and provision in time of need. While some in ministry misuse God's finances, we need to cheerfully support those who work in God's ministry and trust God to deal with those who abuse church finances.

Giving to the Poor

The Bible also directs us to give to the poor in Deuteronomy 15:7–8:

If there is a poor man among your brothers in any of the towns of the land that the Lord your God is giving you, do not be hardhearted or tightfisted toward your poor brother. Rather be openhanded and freely lend him whatever he needs.

In Matthew 25:35–40, Jesus tells us that when we give to the poor we are giving to him:

"For I was hungry and you gave me something to eat, I was thirsty and you gave me something to drink, I was a stranger and you invited me in, I needed clothes and you clothed me, I was sick and you looked after me, I was in prison and you came to visit me."

"Then the righteous will answer him, 'Lord, when did we see you hungry and feed you, or thirsty and give you something to drink? When did we see you a stranger and invite you in, or needing clothes and clothe you? When did we see you sick or in prison and go to visit you?'

"The King will reply, 'I tell you the truth, whatever you did for one of the least of these brothers of mine, you did for me.'"

Do not neglect this great opportunity to help someone in need. Carol and I pray that God will show us how to be more like him in our giving and that he will bring needy people into our lives whom we can help financially.

How Much Should I Give?

As a counselor, I receive many questions about how much to give. "Because we are not under the Old Testament law, should we still give 10%? Is it 10% of the gross or take-home pay?" The New Testament teaches us to give in proportion to the material blessings we receive. It also commands sacrificial giving. I believe you should prayerfully seek God's will about your level of giving, and whatever that amount is, ask him to help you be obedient to that will. Carol and I are convinced that the right level of giving for our family is 10% of our gross income to our local church and various amounts to others as directed by God.

When counseling others, we typically use 10% as a guideline. If a person is not giving 10% currently and is experiencing financial difficulties, I typically do not recommend that they increase their giving. Instead, I suggest that they seek God's guidance in giving some amount regularly. Even if this amount turns out to only be 1%, I have found that God is faithful in meeting people where they are and can bless them because their heart is meeting the intent of the giving principle.

Growing closer to God and turning our finances over to God are the same path. When Christians understand biblical truths about money, they are more likely to become cheerful givers. Our giving is a direct indication of our spiritual maturity. The Bible says God loves a cheerful giver, but I think it also could be said that a cheerful giver loves God.

8

Work

Colossians 3:23–24:

Whatever you do, work at it with all your heart, as working for the Lord, not for men, since you know that you will receive an inheritance from the Lord as a reward. It is the Lord Christ you are serving.

I have heard varied reports that anywhere from 60%–70% of people dislike their work. We spend the majority of our lives working. It is terrible that 70% of people spend the majority of their lives in a place where they are unhappy. God did not intend for man to despise work. God created work before sin entered the world. Therefore, God intended for us to work all along. God created work to build our character while enabling us to provide for our material well-being. Work also is a way of experiencing a more intimate relationship with God and with other people.

Dave Ramsey writes in *Financial Peace*, "Happy and effective people have found a vocation for which they have a natural aptitude and have committed themselves to excellence in that vocation. These are people who have a vacation for a vocation." God has given each of us natural abilities and passions. If we can identify those, we will not only be happier and perform better in that role, but we will also become well paid for it. God gives us all unique skills and abilities. We should not be jealous of others' skills. Working where we are using our skills most effectively indicates that we are doing what God has called us to do.

It is time for you to work hard to excel at your vocation. Colossians 3:23–24 reminds us that we should perform our work as if God is watching because he is:

Whatever you do, work at it with all your heart, as working for the Lord, not for men, since you know that you will receive an inheritance from the Lord as a reward. It is the Lord Christ you are serving.

It does not matter that our employers cannot see that we are slacking off, because we are not working solely for them. We should always strive to work hard and do our best. As Christians, we are to set an example for others. We do not want others to associate Christianity with laziness. Martin Luther King Jr.'s famous street sweeper quote reminds us that God expects excellence in our work:

If a man is called to be a street sweeper, he should sweep streets even as Michelangelo painted, or Beethoven played music, or Shakespeare wrote poetry. He should sweep streets so well that all the hosts of heaven and earth will pause to say, here lived a great street sweeper who did his job well.

What if I Am Not in the Right Vocation?

Revelations 3:7:

What he opens no one can shut, and what he shuts no one can open.

If you are not currently in the right career field, you should begin making plans to move into the career that best fit your abilities and desires. However, *do not quit your job today.* You can begin the process for discovery and transformation without destroying your monthly budget. Even though your current job may not be the best career fit for you, it provides financial means that can help you transition into a long-term career that best meets your abilities and passions. Many resources can help you identify that best career fit. I recommend you read Tim LaHaye's *Why You Act the Way You Do* and Larry Burkett and Lee Ellis's *Finding the Career That Fits You.*

It is worth the time and efforts to invest in finding the best career fit. Even as you begin the discovery process, you should continue working hard at your current job and be careful not to waste or misuse your current employer's resources. Do not spend time on the job planning your transitions. Remember, God placed you there for a purpose. He is expecting you to be faithful to him in your work while watching for open doors. We have to trust God to open the right career doors at the right time.

LaHaye explains in *Why You Act the Way You Do:*

"We just need to stay in close fellowship with the Master, who does have a plan for our lives. So we should busy ourselves cleaning up the room we are now in and God will, in his own time, open another door for us. Once inside, we will find it too needs a lot

of hard work, so we should busy ourselves cleaning up the second room. About the time we get that room cleaned up, there will be a third door open to us, then a fourth and so on. Finally, we will look back and say, 'Hasn't God been faithful to lead us into so many places of opportunity to serve him?' But in the meantime we need to be found faithful, cleaning in the room we are in."

Should Wives Work Outside the Home?

Titus 2:4–5:

Then they can train the younger women to love their husbands and children, to be self-controlled and pure, to be busy at home.

Proverbs 31:10–31:

A wife of noble character who can find?...She brings [her husband] good, not harm, all the days of her life. She selects wool and flax and works with eager hands...She gets up while it is still dark; she provides food for her family...She considers a field and buys it; out of her earnings she plants a vineyard. She sets about her work vigorously...She sees that her trading is profitable, and her lamp does not go out at night. In her hand she holds the distaff and grasps the spindle with her fingers. She opens her arms to the poor and extends her hands to the needy. When it snows, she has no fear for her household; for all of them are clothed in scarlet. She makes coverings for her bed; she is clothed in fine linen and purple. Her husband is respected at the city gate, where he takes his seat among the elders of the land. She makes linen garments and sells them, and supplies the merchants with sashes. She watches over the affairs of her household and does not eat the bread of idleness. Her children arise and call her blessed; her husband also, and he praises her: "Many women do noble things, but you surpass them all." Charm is deceptive, and beauty is fleeting; but a woman who fears the Lord is to be praised. Give her the reward she has earned, and let her works bring her praise at the city gate.

At some point in their marriage, most couples with children face the question, "Should wives work?" Titus 2:4–5 encourages women with small children to limit work outside the home, while Proverbs 31 paints a picture of a working wife living a balanced life with the majority of her activity focused on the home. Some women are gifted as homemakers. Although homemakers sometimes go without honor and proper appreciation, there is no more important job than raising godly children. It is, however, a job that is temporary. As her children get older, the stay-at-home mom enjoys more freedom to pursue work outside the home. Some women have the skills and desire to work outside the home and manage to balance work with family activities. Other women have to work because their income is necessary to provide for their family. In either case, it is a decision that the husband and wife must make prayerfully and with full agreement.

Carol and I decided when our first child was one year old that Carol would become a stay-at-home-mom. Initially, we thought it would be a financial struggle, but we found that the adjustment was much smoother than we had imagined. I am convinced that more couples would choose the same route if they took a more accurate look at the true impact of living on a single income instead of double income. Couples sometimes fail to consider that a second job means additional taxes and giving. A second job also likely results in more transportation, clothing, personal care, childcare, and eating-out expenses. **Table 3** helps place the true impact of a second income into perspective.

Table 3: Net Additional Income from Working Mom

Income and Spending	Example 1	Example 2	Your situation
Wife's gross yearly income	$35,000	$52,000	
Wife's gross weekly income	$673	$1,000	
Wife's expenses			
Giving (10%)	$67	$100	
Federal income taxes (25%)	$168	$250	
State income taxes (10%)	$67	$50	
Social Security tax (7.5%)	$50	$75	
Transportation (10 trips×20 miles×$.25/mile)	$50	$50	
Lunch/snacks/coffee breaks	$15	$15	
Restaurants/convenience food	$35	$35	
Extra clothing/cleaning	$20	$20	
Personal grooming	$5	$5	
Childcare	$140	$140	
Total expenses	$617	$740	
Net additional family income	$58	$260	
Net income per hour	$1.45	$6.50	

Many couples are surprised to see that income from a second job is not as much as they expected. If you are faced with this decision, use the table above to analyze your situation, and then determine as a couple if the added income offsets the effects a working mom's physical and emotional demands have on your family.

Rest

Exodus 34:21 encourages us to take a day to rest:

Six days you shall labor, but on the seventh day you shall rest; even during the plowing season and harvest you must rest.

We should work hard, but not so hard that we do not take time for relationships and rest. I have committed to taking one day a week to do only things that rejuvenate me. I sit in my recliner and watch football, play games with the kids, go out with Carol, or do any other activity that I enjoy. On this day, I do not do yard work, pay bills, check e-mail at work, or do any other work-related activity. It helps me remain peaceful and keeps me ready to work hard the other days of the week.

9

True Riches

Mark 8:36:

What good is it for a man to gain the whole world, yet forfeit his soul?

One day my kids and I were playing the board game Life, in which the winner is the person who retires with the most money. I thought to myself, "That may be how the world keeps score, but that is not so with God." In our culture, we believe we are "winning" when we acquire more and more stuff and money.

People who do not know God look at life as the time between birth and death. It is no surprise when they conclude, "If this is all there is to life, why should I deny myself any pleasures or possessions?" Those who know Christ have a different perspective. We know this life is only a short prelude to an eternal life spent in either heaven or hell.

Eternity is a long time. I am sure I had a few bad days in kindergarten, but at thirty-eight years old, I do not remember them. After being in heaven for a million years, we will not even remember things that happened on earth. Nevertheless, what we do in our short time here determines how we will spend eternity.

Because we realize we are only on this earth for a very short time, Carol and I have committed to live life with a God-centered purpose. We have posted in our home a framed message that reads:

> **<u>Moody Family Mission:</u>**
> **Our mission is to love God, to love**
> **others, and to take good care of the**
> **things that God gives to us.**

As a family, we recite this statement every day before school. We try to incorporate this mission into every aspect of our lives. Our goal is not to live perfect lives, but to live purposeful lives. We believe one day we will all go before God to account for our lives and that we had better have good answer to two questions:

"What did you do with my son, Jesus?"
and
"What did you do with what I gave you?"

At that point on judgment day, nothing else will matter. My college degrees and executive positions will not help me. The car I drive and the home I live in will mean absolutely nothing. It will not matter if I had the wealth of Bill Gates, Donald Trump, and Oprah combined. None of this will be enough to compensate for not having good answers to those two questions. I believe that even though I try to live a God-centered life, I will look back and wonder why I did not do more for God while I lived on earth. Why did I spend so much time worrying about stuff and money?

I wrote this book because I believe God wanted me to use his incredible blessings in my life to help others form a more intimate relationship with him. My responsibility is to share my personal experiences and teach you how to apply God's biblical principles for handling money. I have warned you about the danger of going into debt, given you practical steps to take toward becoming financially free, and encouraged you to have an eternal perspective when it comes to money and possessions.

If you have not done so already, I urge you to consider choosing Jesus as your Lord and Savior today. I am certain that choosing Jesus will be a decision that you will never regret. Salvation is an once-in-a-lifetime decision, but turning over our will to God is a daily commitment.

I am honored that you joined me on your journey to a financial breakthrough. I pray not only that you will prosper financially, but that you will prosper in all aspect of your life. Just as I aim to have an intimate relationship with God, I pray that you will grow closer to God. I also pray that you prosper in your relationships, enjoy good health, and fulfill all your God-given dreams. Thank you for allowing me to share my story and God's message concerning financial stewardship with you.

APPENDIX A

Blank Financial Statement

PERSONAL FINANCIAL STATEMENT		
Date:		
Assets (Current market value)		
	Amount	
Cash on hand/checking account		
Savings		
Stocks and bonds		
Cash value of life insurance		
Home		
Other real estate		
Mortgages/notes receivable		
Business valuation		
Automobiles		
Furniture		
Jewelry		
Other personal property		
Pension/401k/retirement		
Other assets		
Total assets:		
Liabilities (Current amount owed)		
	Amount	
Credit card debt		
Automobile loans		
Home mortgages		
Personal debt to relatives		
Business loans		
Educational loans		
Past due medical bills		
Other past due bills		
Life insurance loans		
Bank loans		
Other debts and loans		
Total liabilities:		
NET WORTH (Total assets minus total liabilities)		

APPENDIX B

Financial Statement Example

PERSONAL FINANCIAL STATEMENT		
Date:	**September 16, 2002**	
Assets (Current market value)		
	Amount	
Cash on hand/checking account	$ 200	
Savings	$ 100	
Stocks and bonds	$0	
Cash value of life insurance	$0	
Home	$ 220,000	
Other real estate	$0	
Mortgages/notes receivable	$0	
Business valuation	$0	
Automobiles	$ 15,000	
Furniture	$ 5,000	
Jewelry	$ 2,000	
Other personal property	$0	
Pension/401k/retirement	$ 7,000	
Other assets	$0	
Total assets:		**$ 249,300**
Liabilities (Current amount owed)		
	Amount	
Credit card debt	$ 53,000	
Automobile loans	$ 1,500	
Home mortgages	$ 203,000	
Personal debt to relatives	$0	
Business loans	$ 4,000	
Educational loans	$ 27,000	
Past due medical bills	$0	
Other past due bills		
Life insurance loans	$0	
Bank loans	$ 2,000	
Other debts and loans	$0	
Total liabilities:		**$ 290,500**
NET WORTH (Total assets minus total liabilities)		**$ (41,200.)**

Appendix C

Blank Debt List

DEBT LIST				
Date:				
	Describe what was purchased	Monthly payment	Balance due	Interest rate
CREDITOR				
TOTALS				
AUTO LOANS				
TOTAL AUTO LOANS				
HOME MORTGAGES				
TOTAL HOME MORTGAGES				
BUSINESS DEBT				
TOTAL BUSINESS DEBT				

APPENDIX D

Debt List Example

DEBT LIST				
Date:	October 1, 2002			
	Describe what was purchased	Monthly payment	Balance due	Interest rate
CREDITOR				
MBNA	Misc.	$300	$18,968	17.99%
Amex	Misc.	$160	$8,000	10.90%
Universal Card	Misc.	$103	$4,985	5.90%
Chase	Misc.	$142	$7,140	9.90%
Juniper Credit Card	Misc.	$24	$1,000	12.00%
Sallie Mae	Student loans	$50	$4,500	5.00%
Wells Fargo	Student loans	$203	$22,128	8.00%
Citi Bank	Misc.	$160	$7,741	12.90%
Wachovia	Carpet	$0	$2,018	0.00%
BOA Overdraft Credit	Misc.	$18	$1,000	18.00%
TOTAL CREDIT CARD		**$1,160**	**$77,480**	
AUTO LOANS				
First Virginia	Minivan	$485	$1,500	9.00%
TOTAL AUTO LOANS		**$485**	**$1,500**	
HOME MORTGAGES				
Bank of America	Home	$1,723	$203,000	6.75%
TOTAL HOME MORTGAGES		**$1,723**	**$203,000**	
BUSINESS DEBT				
Bryde	Accounting fees	$50	$ 1,575	0.00%
Long Aldridge	Legal fees	$50	$ 2,490	0.00%
TOTAL BUSINESS DEBT		**$ 100**	**$ 4,065**	

APPENDIX E

Monthly Spending Log

Month   **Year**

Category Date	Income	Tithe/Giving	Taxes	Housing	Food	Transportation	Insurance
1							
2							
3							
4							
5							
6							
7							
8							
9							
10							
11							
12							
13							
14							
15							
16							
17							
18							
19							
20							
21							
22							
23							
24							
25							
26							
27							
28							
29							
30							
31							
This month actual							

Category Date	Debts	Entertain	Clothing	Savings	Medical	Misc.	Invest	School
1								
2								
3								
4								
5								
6								
7								
8								
9								
10								
11								
12								
13								
14								
15								
16								
17								
18								
19								
20								
21								
22								
23								
24								
25								
26								
27								
28								
29								
30								
31								
This month actual								

APPENDIX F

Suggested Percentage Guidelines for Family Income

GROSS HOUSEHOLD INCOME	$35,000	$45,000	$55,000	$65,000	$85,000	$115,000
1. Tithe/Giving	10.0%	10.0%	10.0%	10.0%	10.0%	10.0%
2. Taxes 1,*	11.2%	14.8%	17.2%	18.8%	23.5%	26.3%
NET SPENDABLE	$27,580	$33,840	$40,040	$46,280	$56,525	$73,255
3. Housing	36.0%	32.0%	30.0%	30.0%	30.0%	29.0%
4. Food	12.0%	13.0%	12.0%	11.0%	11.0%	11.0%
5. Transportation	12.0%	13.0%	14.0%	14.0%	13.0%	13.0%
6. Insurance	5.0%	5.0%	5.0%	5.0%	5.0%	5.0%
7. Debts	5.0%	5.0%	5.0%	5.0%	5.0%	5.0%
8. Entertainment/Recreation	5.0%	5.0%	7.0%	7.0%	7.0%	8.0%
9. Clothing	5.0%	5.0%	6.0%	6.0%	7.0%	7.0%
10. Savings	5.0%	5.0%	5.0%	5.0%	5.0%	5.0%
11. Medical/Dental	6.0%	6.0%	5.0%	5.0%	5.0%	5.0%
12. Miscellaneous	4.0%	6.0%	6.0%	7.0%	7.0%	7.0%
13. Investments 2	5.0%	5.0%	5.0%	5.0%	5.0%	5.0%
14. School/Child Care 3	6.0%	5.0%	5.0%	5.0%	5.0%	5.0%

1. Guideline percentages for tax category include taxes for Social Security, federal, and a small estimated amount for state, based on 2002 rates. The tax code changes regularly. Please be sure to insert your actual tax into this category.
2. This category is used for long-term investment planning, such as college education or retirement.
3. This category is added as a guide only. If you have this expense, the percentage shown must be deducted from other budget categories.
* In some cases earned income credit will apply. It may be possible to increase the number of deductions to lessen the amount of tax paid per month. Review the last tax return for specific information.

** This spreadsheet is a modified version of Crown Financial Ministry's suggested percentage guidelines for a family of three to four.

APPENDIX G

Estimated Budget Worksheet (blank)

Estimated Budget Worksheet				
	Column A	Column B	Column C	Column D
Monthly income				
	Monthly Spending tracking	Suggested spending from guidelines	Variance	New estimated budget
GROSS MONTHLY INCOME				
LESS				
Category 1 – Tithe/giving				
Category 2 – Taxes				
NET SPENDABLE INCOME				
Monthly living expenses				
Category 3–Housing (total)				
Category 4–Food				
Category 5–Transportation				
Category 6–Insurance				
Category 7–Debts				
Category 8–Entertainment				
Category 9–Clothing				
Category 10–Savings				
Category 11–Medical				
Category 12–Miscellaneous				
Category 13–Investments				
Category 14–School/childcare				
Total expenses				
INCOME vs. LIVING EXPENSES				
Net spendable income				
Less total expenses				
Surplus or deficit				

APPENDIX H

Estimated Budget Worksheet (sample)

Estimated Budget Worksheet (sample)				
	Column A	Column B	Column C	Column D
Monthly Income				
	Monthly Spending tracking	Suggested spending from guideline	Variance	New Estimated Budget
GROSS MONTHLY INCOME	$7,036	$7,036	$7,036	$7,036
LESS				
Category 1–Tithe/giving	$704	$704	$0	$704
Category 2–Taxes	$1,639	$1,639	$0	$1,639
NET SPENDABLE INCOME	$4,693	$4,693		$4,693
Monthly Living Expenses				
Category 3–Housing (total)	$1,826	$1,408	-$418	$1,354
Category 4–Food	$287	$516	$229	$267
Category 5–Transportation	$309	$610	$301	$152
Category 6–Insurance	$0	$235	$235	$248
Category 7–Debts	$1,644	$235	-$1,409	$1,390
Category 8–Entertainment	$498	$328	-$170	$200
Category 9–Clothing	$0	$328	$328	$40
Category 10–Savings	$502	$235	-$267	$500
Category 11–Medical	$620	$235	-$385	$50
Category 12–Miscellaneous	$60	$328	$268	$250
Category 13–Investments	$244	$235	-$9	$242
Category 14–School/childcare	$0	$0	$0	$0
Total expenses	$5,990	$4,693	-$1,297	$4,693
INCOME vs. LIVING EXPENSES				
Net spendable income	$4,693	$4,693		$4,693
Less total expenses	$5,990	$4,693		$4,693
Surplus or Deficit	-$1,297	$0		$0

Bibliography

Bach, David. *The Automatic Millionaire: A Powerful One-Step Plan to Live and Finish Rich*. New York: Broadway Books, 2004.

Blue, Ron. *The Debt Squeeze: How Your Family Can Become Financially Free*. Nashville, Tennessee: W Publishing Group, 1989.

Dayton, Howard. *Your Money Counts: The Biblical Guide to Learning, Spending, Saving, Investing, Giving, and Getting Out of Debt*. Wheaton, Illinois: Tyndale House, 1997.

Jet Magazine, *"Why Money Is the Leading Cause of Divorce."* November 18, 1996.

Kiyosaki, Robert T. *Rich Dad, Poor Dad*. New York: Warner Books, 2000.

LaHaye, Tim. *Why You Act the Way You Do*. Tyndale House, 1988.

New International Version Quest Study Bible, Revised. Grand Rapids, Michigan: Zondervan, 2003.

Orman, Suze. *The 9 Steps to Financial Freedom*. New York: Crown, 1997.

Ramsey, Dave. *Financial Peace: Revisited*. New York: Viking Books, 2002.

Stanley, Thomas J. and William D. Danko. *The Millionaire Next Door*. New York: Longstreet Press, 1996.

Warren, Rick. *The Purpose-driven Life: What on Earth Am I Here For?*. Grand Rapids, Michigan: Zondervan, 2002.

Warren, Rick, and John Baker. *Celebrate Recovery*. Grand Rapids, Michigan: Zondervan, 1998.

Wilkinson, Bruce. *The Dream Giver*. Sisters, Oregon: Multnomah, 2003.

About the Author

Travis Moody was born in Memphis, Tennessee. He attended Georgia Tech on football scholarship and graduated with a Bachelor of Science in Industrial Engineering. He later obtained an MBA from Duke University's Fuqua School of Business. He has spent over 15 years as a manager and executive with Fortune 500 companies in South Carolina, Washington, Georgia, Tennessee, and Arkansas.

Travis is a certified Money Map Coach. He implemented Crown Financial Ministry programs at churches in both Tennessee and Arkansas. He has led Crown Financial Ministry small-group studies, delivered financial stewardship messages to congregations, and served couples as a financial counselor.

Travis has been married to his wonderful wife, Carol, for over 17 years and is the proud father of two girls, Erica and Gilana, and two boys, Travis Jr. and Donovan. He and his family reside in Cordova, Tennessee.